A Life Well Lived

by

John Paul Vialard

Dedicated to

My Loving Family

Acknowledgments

A Life Well Lived is a gift to my family. It couldn't have been done without the help of many, who I would like to acknowledge here.

Skylands RSVP & Volunteer Resource Center, in connection with Northwest NJ Community Action Program Inc. (NORWESCAP), links the skills of volunteers with local organizations. Sharon Palmer is the volunteer who runs NORWESCAP's Lifebook program. She feels that "nobody's life is boring," and she recruited volunteers to prove it. The volunteers work with seniors to record their life experiences for their families.

My good friend, Pat Addison, connected me to the Life Book program, and got the ball rolling.

Scott Moore is the volunteer who was assigned to my story, and we collaborated regularly over many months. The final compilation of the book was accomplished by Sharon Palmer, who designed the cover and put everything into book format.

Finally, my daughter and son-in-law, Joan and Richard Renton, have spent many hours reviewing, proofing, and editing to bring the project to fruition.

I thank them all, and I am grateful for their interest and help.

My name is John Paul Vialard and this is my story:

I'll start out with my birth date. I was born in Denville, New Jersey, Cedar Lake section on September 20th, 1918. I got married in 1939 to Evelyn May Ernst. My mother and father were born in France. My father served in the military in France when he turned 21. My father spent three years in the French Army in Africa. Military service was mandatory. They came to the United States separately, they didn't know each other. They both settled in Denville around 1912 or 1913. They bought lakefront property.

I learned to drive on a 1912 Model T Ford. A friend and I found it lying on its side in the woods. We turned it over, fixed it up and I decided I was going to learn how to drive. I drove it dodging in the woods to avoid the trees and think that's what made me a good driver all of these years. I have loved driving and learned every back road and best hunting areas.

I had different jobs. I drove taxi in Denville. I drove quite a few taxis. I started driving taxi at seventeen years old. I had to be seventeen to get a driver's license.

I was in the Civilian Conservation Corps (CCC) in 1936. I was a Forestry Truck Driver in Denville, New Jersey. We helped to make many of the great State Parks of today. I was a chauffeur in 1939 and held other various jobs.

We lived in various places but eventually settled on Foster Road and Broad Street in Denville. We lived there with our children Joan Suzanne and John Albert.

There was a friend of mine, and we had another friend that was a barber in Denville. He wanted to give our other friend a message that the barber had asked him for. I didn't want to go at first, but my friend told me that we would only be there for a few minutes. We went up into where they were having a dance. They opened the door and I looked across the room, and there was a girl watching the other people dance. She was waiting for a partner, who was dancing with her friend's sister. I spotted her, and like a magnet, or a cyclone, I went through all the dancers directly to her. God must have sent her. I went over there and talked with her. At once, I told her that I was going to marry her. Afterward, I asked her where she lived. I asked her for her telephone number so I could call her. She gave me the number and I wrote it down. A couple of days later I called her. I knew where she worked, but I didn't disturb her there. I called her and asked her for a date. She asked to go to the movies. We went to the movies, which was our first date. This was in 1937 at Egbert's lake in Rockaway Township. There was a dance hall there. They called it a lake, but it wasn't that big. They had a few buildings around there. Now the township owns a playground there, and they've taken most of those bungalows down many years ago.

We got married on September 30th, 1939. Shortly after that, we moved back to Denville and I went to work for Hercules Powder Company to help make ammunition. I worked at Hercules which was in Kenvil, New Jersey. There was a big explosion there. The day of the explosion I chanced to take the day off, and went fishing in Hackettstown. We worked seven days a week no days off, and on that day I had such a severe headache that I needed the day off even though I could lose my job. When I heard the explosion, I knew that it was Hercules. I immediately rushed to help.

Before the Hercules explosion, in 1926, the Denmark Naval Ammunition Storage (which is now Picatinny Arsenal) where they also manufactured missiles, they had a big explosion that was caused by lightning. The explosion killed some Marines. They used to call it Lake Denmark Naval Ammunition Storage. They also manufactured the powder for cannons. I remember hearing the explosion when I was eight years old. Every time there was a thunder and lightning storm, I headed for home, thinking of that explosion. The lightning hit the magazine where they stored the explosives they manufactured before they were shipped out, causing the explosion.

My daughter Joan Suzanne was born on the 15th of June in 1943. About a month later, when I had already signed up I got a rating for the Navy. When I was in the Navy, I was with the Navy Seabees. We were like the Army Engineers. I went in to the Seabees with a rating of Carpenter's Mate, and I switched over to a Machinist's Mate, Second Class. When I first went into the Seabees, I went to New York and they turned me down because of my teeth. They either needed to be pulled or filled. I had that taken care of and I went back and they accepted me. That was 1943. I enlisted in New York. After I enlisted there I went down to Virginia for training. We did combat training with the Marines. In Virginia we went through the maneuvers of getting prepared, climbing nets, up and down, and over the fence and under the fence, crawling, throwing hand grenades, target shooting, a lot of marching too. It was good for us. You woke up early in the morning or night and you were in a group and you did PT, it was good for us. We did push ups. After I left Virginia I went to Port Hueneme, Oxnard, California up through New Mexico. While I was there I got injured. I went to the Naval Hospital in Washington.

I stayed at the hospital in Washington. When we went to Portland, Oregon, we had to go between box cars of the train to get to where we needed to eat. It was likely from a brake sliver from the train between the cars that flew up and hit me in the left eye. It kept watering badly, and then both eyes were watering so I couldn't see anything. They telegraphed ahead and had two eye doctors meet us in Portland, Oregon. The doctors said they couldn't do anything and that I needed to go on to the Naval Hospital in Seattle, Washington. The hospital had certain clinics for special problems. Many of those people in the eye ward were even younger than me, had lost their sight all together, or were badly injured and lost their sight in one eye. When I arrived at the hospital I was strapped down on the table so I couldn't move my head, or anything. After they performed the procedure, they told me that they thought they had "got it all". They didn't have the equipment at that time to take pictures where it would show up. I had got something in my eyes, but we weren't sure if it was from the brake shoes of the train when they were going down the mountain. I was there about a week, and all I could see through the left eye was a little peep hole. I have had problems with that eye all my life. When the other eye got better, they took the mask off of me. There was a chaplain that came and talked to me. He was in the service too. I told him that I wanted to catch up to my outfit. The chaplain went and talked to the commanding officer that arranged this, who agreed. They sent me out of the hospital and flew me to Kodiak Island, Alaska, and then from there I went to Adak Island. I flew into Dutch Harbor; from there I took a tanker to go further westward to Attu.

I joined the 138th Battalion on Attu. I had the job of overseer and dispatcher of vehicles and saved them a lot of time. There I worked on the airport on the island. We worked on the runways, and there was plenty of snow. There was an A-Frame, no fancy hydraulic lifts like today, and there were no plows, but they did have big snow blowers. The big snow blowers cleared the runway of the snow. We were having a lot of trouble with accidents, because there were drag lines in the ocean and there was black sand washing in on the beach. They were using mats that we put down that would raise up and have sand between them. I made a suggestion, since we were always having accidents, that we should have a course to teach them how they should be driving and how to put the mats together, which were about six feet long, and we jacked them up with the A-Frame in front of the vehicle. I suggested that we should do it the opposite of what we were doing. We should run along the side so they could keep up with the sand, bring it in, and not run on the mats until they were ready to start lifting it up. I never dreamed what I said to them would be carried through. I didn't realize that when I made the suggestion that I would be the one in charge! They took my suggestion that they should plow this stuff away from the runway because it was getting full of holes. That is where I got my next rating but I also got my job of dispatching and inspecting the trucks as they went out. We worked sixteen hours a day or night, whichever was called for us to be out there. I was discharged. We had a saying, "We'll be in Frisco Bay by the end of May," and it worked out that way. It was May, 1945, and I was home to see my daughter for the first time around her second or third birthday. My wife and daughter were living with her mother and two sisters in Dover, New Jersey.

(Regarding Morris Canal) There were about six or seven crossings across the canal. They were all wooden. They had a canal basin to keep the boats overnight and feed their horses and mules that pulled the canal boats. They crossed the Rockaway River on a viaduct. The only thing I recall about the crossings was that they were all wooden except one. One was a walkover bridge. Prior to that, the only place you could get across was over the viaduct when the boats were being towed past the rest of the area. At the junction at Peer's Store, there was a lock. E.C. Peer was the lock tenant on the canal at the E.C. Peer Store. My mother and I used to go down to Peer's Store. It was the only store around at that time, in that area.

When they got to Peer's Lock, there was a basin near Diamond Spring Road and there was a viaduct. The only time I ever saw the boat on there was when they were surveying to put the sewage line through Denville. In later years, when the buses came in, the canal went bankrupt, due to other forms of transportation. In 1925 there was no longer traffic on the canal.

Then, transportation was by trolley, to get anywhere of any distance. The trolleys were called Morris County Traction Company.

In Denville there was the Wayside stop, which must have been from back in the days of the open coaches. One branch of the Junction went to the Boonton area and on down into Jersey City. The other branch went through Morristown and went through Passaic and other places like that.

I saw them surveying and I remember seeing the surveyor boat tied up on the Cedar Lake side of Denville *(they used to call it Denville Road)*. Before my time, it was called Cranberry Pond.

The Car Barn later became Lakeland Bus in Dover. In Denville one branch went to Morristown and the other toward the Rockaway River. The Denville Line went by Bush's Farm off

Norris Road, and the Convent of the Sisters on Pocono Road, and branched off past Bush's Farm and into Mountain Lakes and Boonton Township.

I rode on most of those trolleys to Morristown and to All Souls Hospital in Morristown. There was no other hospital in the area where I lived at that time. I wasn't born there, I was born at home. We had a property on the lake which we only used for fishing, mostly. It had a beach.

When Denville first got their fire truck, I think it was 1926, but I don't think it was delivered at that time. It was later that I saw that truck for the first time. They were pumping water to demonstrate to the people. They went to every lake in Denville. They wanted to show how far they could shoot the water. They siphoned water from the lakes. The truck was first housed at a makeshift garage, made of some timbers. The man that owned the garage was Horace Cook, Sr. He had a pretty good size family.

That was something about Denville; they had different

areas, different school places, like Union Hill and Shongum Areas – which bordered on Randolph Township and Morris Township. The area we are right now (Morris View Healthcare Center, Morris Township, NJ), the nursing home, was called Shongum Sanitarium. It was a tubercular hospital. My wife Evelyn's father died there in 1936, I believe.

The Wayside Inn was for the carriages. It was at the corner of what is now Main Street and Route 53. It was a stagecoach stop. The Wayside Inn was a famous hotel that burned to the ground in 1953. I was the First Assistant Fire Chief. Charles Ergenzinger was the Fire Chief. I was the first to the fire. I lived on Harriman Avenue at that time.

Denville Junction was interesting because of the two different trolley lines. In later years one went through Dover and Hopatcong for water for the canal. They built a dam so they could get water. You can still see what they did there to get around the mountain leading to Ledgewood and Lake Hopatcong. They raised the dam so they could get enough water to get further down to Ledgewood. If you look real close when you go on Route 80, or go to Landing, you can see the stonework and they must have had to cut those stones. They had to lay the stones that way in order to keep the water in. I don't know how they did that. There wasn't any truck that could bring anything but sand and lime. They couldn't use cement; they didn't have the equipment that they have today.

In 1947 I was Captain of the Rescue Squad and also the First Assistant Fire Chief. I became Fire Chief in 1954, following Chief Ergenzinger. I am now a lifetime member of the Denville Fire Department and am also Denville's oldest past Fire Chief. I was also a Denville Auxiliary Policeman.

In Denville across from the Wayside Inn, Joe Cisco owned the stop where the trolleys branched off toward Rockaway Township, and the other one toward Boonton area and on down. Where the St. Francis Home is now, that belonged to the nuns, and on Diamond Spring Road, that convent was by itself then. I saw it when they were building St. Francis Health Resort. The nuns were out there, and they raised their own food, mostly. They had all their own facilities. They had a bakery inside the place, and they worked in the fields. I remember seeing them in later years. They also had a large orchard where St. Clare's Hospital is today. They had just about every animal you could imagine. They raised most of their food, and they owned a lot of land at that time. They made delicious pastries and rolls for people that came there on their vacation. When they built the big extension, they called it a health resort. When they did that, they had to use the land to build the place they were going to rent out to the people, especially during the summer time. The people would come by train, and then be transported by taxi. They had to give up some of their land for that purpose, to build that building along Diamond Spring Road and Pocono Road and it went over to the golf course. (In later years I caddied on that golf course.) Now they're still being rented out as a health resort. The nuns worked in the fields, they fed the animals, they took care of the animals, they were always working after they opened that. You go off of

Pocono Road, to Norris Road, past the golf course, there is a cemetery at the eighth hole going out on your left going north northwest and a lot of people don't even know that it's there. Speaking of cemeteries, there's one over in Union Hill near where Sonny Danielson used to live, on Cooper Road. At St. Francis, they used to make their own wine. They had the fire department over every year and served wine. When I drove cab, I used to take some of the luggage from the train station. I used to get 25 cents for each trip.

My family and I were all hunters and fishermen. From the time I was eight years old, I was already trapping and skinning the animals. We had a fur buyer that came by once a week from Valley Spring and bought all our furs. When he got the furs that I had trapped, he started to bring the other furs he had bought from other people. He gave me fifteen pelts to skin, and gave me fifteen cents to skin them. When I got older, the fur trader asked if I could clean other skins, because I did such a good job. He was impressed how well I cleaned the pelts. My father and older brother hunted and trapped. One day I went down to the pond where I saw my brother setting a trap. I saw him set the trap, but I didn't realize that he reached under the trap to spring and set the trap. I went over there and put my hand right in the trap, I thought that was what he had done. When I hit the pedal, it got my hand. I was out there screaming. My mother came down and she got me out of the trap. We laughed about it later, but it wasn't a pleasant thing at the time, but I learned a valuable lesson. I was six or seven years old at that time. We lived over by Cedar Lake.

When I went to school, I went along the canal.

In later years I trapped on a floating island in Denville. It got anchored on the ground finally, and it grew roots. When it got very windy, you could walk to that island, it would move. In later years, it had moved where it got stuck. There were two of them, one on the north end of the lake, and another on the south end of Cedar Lake. It had cranberries on that island. There was a man there, my brother, and in later years me, would go on those islands to cover our traps. We trapped muskrats.

My mother and I, when I was small, used to pick wild strawberries. They were as big as my thumb, not like the store bought ones. I don't buy the ones in the store, because they don't taste like anything. I used to help her when she made jelly and preserves for the wintertime. I helped her make grape jelly. She taught me how to bake and cook. She never used a cup for measurement; she showed me how to do it. You put your hand a certain way, into a cup. If you took flour that was in her hand, it would be an exact amount of a cup. She was a very good baker, and a very good cook, because she had done it since she was young. I used to go with her shopping. In later years, she would send me to the store, and I would do the shopping. I would go to the Peer's store, or get on the trolley and go down to Rockaway or Boonton. They had stores then. Peer's store, the building is still there on Diamond Spring Road.

They had drained the canal completely, only in certain areas. You could see the evidence of the canal base. You could see where they fed the animals that pulled the canal boats. They went along the tow path. One horse could probably pull a canal boat. Surveyors came all the way from the Delaware River, on the Jersey Side, probably to Jersey City; they were surveying to see where they were going to run the sewer line. The animals had a thing over their mouth to hold the food. We would walk along the canal tow path to get to Peer's Store on Diamond Spring Road to get food.

When we went down to Peer's Store, they sold a twenty-five pound bag of flour. If there was snow on the ground, you would put your groceries on the sled. There were no plastic bags then. They would put your groceries in heavy paper, not bags, along with feed for the animals at home and other things.

We had rabbits, we had geese. My older brother built a large cage. We used to eat rabbits and goat meat. My mother used to make cottage cheese from the goats, and strained it through cheesecloth to get the water out of it. It was very tasty. I used to love duck eggs omelet. We ate tame rabbits, pigeons and rice. We canned a lot of food. When my daughter Joan came along, she would sit on the goats. She loved them and loved to drink the goat milk.

The nuns that had the convent, in later years, they graded the ground and they built St. Francis Health Resort. My mom used to do some laundry for the residents that came out to stay for the summer, usually a couple of weeks, sometimes a month. You wouldn't see them during the wintertime; they were just there for vacation. They would be gone when it got cold weather. The nuns decided to expand. The convent owned the property where St. Clair's Hospital is now. When they expanded they built the resort in front of it, on Diamond Spring Road. They had their own bakery. When I was driving cab in Denville, I would take peoples' luggage inside, and on my way out, it never failed, I got pastries and goodies from the nuns. I got more out of those nuns than I did for driving that cab. I used to get a quarter per person for each person in the taxi. They always gave a bigger tip than the fare. If you could get six people in the vehicle... back then there were different make cars, most of them were touring cars, there were no windows in them, only isinglass. I don't know where that came from, because there was no plastic, it wasn't like the regular glass you looked through, it was just to protect you from the rain. The nuns made their own wine. When prohibition ended, they were still making wine, but they weren't selling it; they were serving it. My mom used to leave me when I was little with the Peer girls that lived about a quarter of a mile from us. She would go over to the St. Francis Health Resort and get the laundry. Back then they had enclosed collars that needed a lot of starch. They would hook together, similar to a tie today. She had to wash them with a scrubbing board and iron them. We didn't have running water. We had two wells we got water from, hand dug.

My mom and I picked beautiful strawberries. We picked nuts; there were all kinds of nuts then. There were beautiful nuts. Some of those chestnut trees died. Some of them were at least five foot across at the bottom. My dad used to find them, and with a hand chisel used to clean them out on the inside and make bee hives out of them. In the summer, when the bees were flying around, they would gather the pollen, and keep doing that, and generate the procedure of nature. My dad only took a little bit of honey out of those hives. I used to help him, at a distance. He'd walk there and he had bees all around him. They never bothered him except one time. My mother counted about up to forty bee stings on him. It wasn't the bees that bothered me so much; I got bit up by mosquitoes. Our family worked together. I picked berries and put them in a glass jar, blueberries, strawberries, and nuts: hazelnuts, filbert nuts, and butter nuts. I could only carry about six quart jars. They've disappeared. Walnuts, they're still around. Pesticides have destroyed many things.

We survived. We had the animals. It was tough times sometimes. We ate a lot of dried beans. We ate some of the pigeons, with rice, and canned that stuff. That's the way we lived.

The house inside had a kitchen where we ate. There was a porch next to the stove, and the porch in later years was glassed in. In the summer, the glass slid between the tracks. In the wintertime, my mother used to take the goose down and make a mattress out of the feathers. She put six inch round pieces of hickory in my bed with that nice down mattress, the same way with a pillow and a stocking cap that she knitted. We would buy one ton of chestnut coal. The rest of it was wood. We had five acres of land on one side of the road, later my brothers and I split up three parts of the land there, and we had a lakefront lot.

One day my father was right along side the dock fishing with a cane pole. He had caught a big pickerel. He threw the used bait over the top of a boat on the dock. I was standing on the dock, and I tried to reach down to get it, and fell in the water, and down to the bottom. He heard a splash; he thought I had thrown something in. He called me and didn't see me. He called a couple more times, and got out of the boat, and up on the dock. He kept calling. He looked down and saw me on the bottom of the lake, holding onto something. He jumped right in and got me. I was about five or six years old at that time. Soon after that I learned how to swim!

I had two brothers. I never saw my sister, who was born in France. My sister's name was Suzane Marie. My oldest brother Al he was born in France. My brother Henry and I were born at Cedar Lake, by a midwife. I was the youngest son.

My father was in the French Army, when you were twenty-one you had to serve three years in the French Army. He went to Africa. When he got out of Africa, he went to one of his uncles. My father just missed the 1912 San Francisco earthquake. He went to San Francisco to visit his uncle. He went back to New York then boarded a ship to France. After that, he went to New York to work for a wine distributor. My parents went back to France after getting married in New York. My parents came from France in the 1800's, and they met in New York. They both worked for wine distributors in this country but not the same company. It was legal then. They imported wine from the vineyards in France. One vineyard was in Orangeburg. The reason why my mother and father met, when it came time to eat, they met at the table during meals. They talked to each other, and that's how they met. Eventually, they got to know each other. Neither one of them was thinking about getting married right away. They got to know who they were and where they came from in France. They didn't come from the same part of France. My father came from Cransac Dept. Aveyron in the South of France; my mother came from the North of France. After a few visits there, they decided to get married. A counselor, like a social worker, and the nuns made the arrangements. They got married in New York City, and then they went back to France. My sister Suzane was born in France. My parents traveled several times to and from France, leaving my sister in France under the care of someone there. When they returned to France, they were told that Suzane had died. No one knows what had happened to her. They took their word. We never knew what happened to Suzane.

When my great-grandmother died, my grandfather inherited the farm. My mother's father was always playing the big shot, and when his wife (my grandmother) died, he didn't take care of the farm. He didn't take care of it at all. He didn't have any interest in farming, and all he wanted to do was "bend the elbow" with his buddies in town.

After my grandmother (mother's mother) died, my grandfather (mother's father) lost the farm, and he went to the convent and left my mother there. He was boozing it up with his buddies, not paying any attention; the money ran out, he lost the farm. So he took her to the convent and they took her in.

My mother was about ten or twelve years old when she was sent to the convent. When she was eighteen, she left the convent and went to work for a family that owned a French winery. She worked for the distributor in New York City. My mother was in Nyack, and my father was in Orangeburg in New York.

After they had gotten married, they had my baby sister, and wanted to come back to the United States and wanted to get hired by somebody else. From New York, they worked for another French woman, a dress maker and designer. She had a place in New York and had people working for her. Denville was this French woman's summer place. When she moved back to France, my father and mother decided to stay in Denville. That's why they ended up in Denville. The woman had a brother that wanted to be a big shot and wanted a chicken farm; which went bust.

When they moved to Denville, my father mainly worked on stonework and masonry. He built fish pools for fancy fish, and took care of them. Then he worked on most of the lakes that were built in Denville. He also helped to make Lake Mohawk in Sussex County. Most of the lakes were owned by a company called A.B. Crane and Company. I think they were the ones that actually developed Broadway in Denville, the actual final stages. They built good size homes back then. He worked a lot in Mountain Lakes. He moved around.

My father's brother and father were coal miners in France. My father never had any desire to be a miner. He spent three years mandatory in Africa in the French Military. He got situated in Denville, and they stayed there until he died.

I had some very good friends, very, very close. Most of them are all buried now. One friend comes to visit me now. He has a farm up in New York State. He was a basketball coach for Jefferson Girls Basketball. He was doing everything for me. I got banged up pretty good a few times, and he would take my garbage out, if it snowed, he would clean my car off. His name is Jim O'Connor.

Another very close friend of mine was Sonny Danielson. He lived in Dover. He was the Section Fire Warden. He got me into the state Forest Fire Service and got me my commission through him. That's how I got into the New Jersey Forest Fire Service. I was a District Fire Warden at Large. That was back in 1947. He had a boat down in Brielle that could sleep five people. Joan was there and my wife Evelyn. My son Jack went deep sea fishing with me and the guys. Evelyn, Joan and Ruth (Sonny's wife) enjoyed the beach.

I belong to the Masonic Lodge, a Master Mason. I'm also

a 32nd Degree Mason and also a Shriner. I had so many jobs I couldn't attend meetings that much. I belonged to that, starting in 1954, when I became Fire Chief.

As far as the Denville Fire Department, around that time, I was also the First Aid Captain of the Rescue Squad, and also a fireman at Picatinny Arsenal and shifted over to doing the millwright work and went into hydraulics; installing them and also repairing them. Some of the parts they made, when I was working there, were used during World War II. Later, I became a Special Fire Warden for Denville Township.

As far as friends go, I had many of them. Lots of them I helped, and lots of them helped me when I needed it. I got along with everybody.

I worked as a carpenter for a while. That was another good friend, Russ Lash. I left him to go to Picatinny, because I had benefits, because I didn't have any benefits with him. In the wintertime, we didn't have any construction going because you always waited for good weather. He said to me, if you promise me that you'll be here in the spring, working for me, then I'll keep you on all winter; and he did. He was starting a development, and I went to work for him. When I was off of Picatinny, so many days a week, I would work for him. Mostly, laying hardwood floors. Everything worked out pretty good.

Bill Covert was a retired Denville Township police officer. We hunted and fished together in Delaware and Sullivan Counties, in New York State. I was at his cabin several times. We saw each other a lot. He was one of the last closest friends to go, and I miss him a lot. I sometimes see his son, which brings back many memories.

Another good friend, Pat Addison, a past Denville Fire Chief, keeps me informed and updated about the department. We have gotten to know each other well and I appreciate everything he does for me.

For vacation, we used to go all over. We went to parks, down the shore and on picnics. We took our family to Canada. I've been in Canada fishing, in Quebec, with friends. We camped on an island in an Indian reservation. In fact, we had an Indian guide. Sonny Danielson and I, we had a guide that took us from one lake to the other. We had a good size canoe. The guide had the outboard motor, Danielson in the middle, and me in the front. Something happened to the motor. One island looked the same as the other to me. We had some paddles, in case something happened so we could get to shore. The mosquitoes and black flies were driving us crazy. Well, he cleaned the plugs, and probably put a couple of new plugs in it, and pretty soon we started out, and the guide pointed and said "moose". There was a moose there swimming. When we spotted the moose, the guide steered toward it. He got there along side the moose that was swimming, and I was in the front. I thought we were just going to look at it. The guide told me to hit it in the nose. So Danielson had swapped himself a full-size axe for a camp axe. He was in the middle of the canoe, and when he got alongside the moose, he hit the moose between the antlers, and the moose just went "woof" just like that. We got near an island, and we couldn't pull the moose out of the lake, it was so huge. I didn't go with them when they cut it up and put it in the two canoes. I stayed back at the camp and cleaned up when they went back and cleaned up the moose. It was legal for the Indians to get the moose, but not us. We didn't take the moose out, we left it at the reservation, and the Indians got it.

I had many fishing stories: deep sea, and almost all the lakes. I used to net bait through the ice and wholesale it, and also delivered it. It was hard work after my regular jobs. I had too many jobs. That's what happened to the knees. I guess the average person and all good people have things happen to them.

About my family:

We have two children, Joan Suzanne and John Albert. Joan and her husband, Richard, have two daughters, Lisa and Sandra. Lisa, her four sons, Jacob, Ben, Eli, Caleb, and their father, Kelly. Sandra and her husband Jim have two children, Kaitlyn and James. Son John Albert and wife Linda, his sons David and Daniel. Their mother, Irene. David and wife Olaya have a daughter, Evelyn Claire, named after her great grandmother.

My son also became a hunter when he was young. He got his first buck where the Union Hill stores on Rte. 10 are now. That was about fifty years ago. We also enjoyed fishing together and were Denville's only peanut farmers in the 1950's. Our son was in Viet Nam where he got a purple heart. I call my son Jocko. My daughter became a Licensed Practical Nurse and was a Pre-School Director and Nurse in Andover Township. We are a close family and have deep love for each other.

On September 30, 2012 we celebrated our seventy-third wedding anniversary. I love her more today than ever. There are so many memories, happy memories, of our children, grandchildren and great grandchildren. We reside together at Morris View Health Care Center. We continue to meet wonderful people and make new friends. We are thankful for the devotion of the staff that cares for us daily and we are always very happy to see our loving family and friends. I love my family and the friends I had, and have now. My life is a good one, with so many good times and good people. The only problem is that it is all going too fast.

John – June, 1925

Evelyn, John & Joan – August, 1943

John – November, 1944

Evelyn, Joan & John – June, 1945

John & Evelyn – December, 1948

John & Jack – 1948

Evelyn & John – October 1, 2008
Forever in Love

John (glasses) – Memorial Day Parade – 2010

Made in the USA
Charleston, SC
07 January 2013